Fantastic
Farm
Machines

Fantastic Farm Machines

by Cris Peterson

Photographs by David R. Lundquist

BOYDS MILLS PRESS

Text copyright © 2006 by Cris Peterson

Photographs copyright © 2006 by David R. Lundquist

All rights reserved

Published by Boyds Mills Press, Inc.

A Highlights Company

815 Church Street

Honesdale, Pennsylvania 18431

Printed in China

CIP data is available

Visit our Web site at www.boydsmillspress.com

First edition, 2006

Book design by Amy Drinker, Aster Designs

The text of this book is set in Minion and Americana.

10 9 8 7 6 5 4 3 2 1

For Gary, my farm machinery expert
and very best friend
—C. P.

To my late father, John, who introduced me to
the creativity and enjoyment of photography
—D. R. L.

When Grandpa farmed with horses and one-bottom plows, it was tough, back-breaking work. So when the first tractors became available, Grandpa bought one right away. He loved farm machinery.

Today our family uses all kinds of machines to help us farm—tractors and planters, choppers and chisel plows. We have a special machine for almost every job we do.

Tractor

Tractors are the most important machines on our farm. We have an old tractor we use for grading the road. We use another tractor with eight huge wheels for field work. It is so fast and powerful that it can pull a plow through an acre of land in less than five minutes. The wheel wells are so big you can almost stand in them.

A chisel plow turns the soil over to the sunshine. It is pulled behind our biggest tractor and helps make the fields ready for planting. Everyone in our family loves to plow because the earth smells so good and we can imagine the crops growing as we work.

Chisel

Plow

Years ago we had to plow, and then disk, and then dig, and then drag each field before we could plant it. We bounced and bumped along on our tractors for days. Now we have a soil finisher. It cuts up the clods of soil and smooths out the seedbed so the ground looks like a perfect brown carpet. Our crops grow green and lush in fields dug with the soil finisher.

Soil

Finisher

Our corn planter plants twelve rows of perfectly spaced seeds at a time. It is pulled by a tractor that has a computer to show us exactly how much seed we are using per acre. Each tiny kernel, or seed, travels through a maze of metal disks and tubes until it drops into the ground. A packing wheel then covers the seed with dirt.

Corn

Planter

Grain

Our grain drill plants wheat, oats, soybeans, and other crops. The tiny seeds sift through metal plates and plastic tubes to land in narrow, nearly invisible rows in the soil. Instead of separate, wide rows like the ones the corn planter makes, we end up with an unbroken blanket of green plants.

Drill

Irrigation

An irrigation pivot sprays thousands of gallons of water onto a circle of plants up to a half-mile wide. With its silvery tubing and long, arching arms, this machine looks like the skeleton wing of a huge prehistoric bird. When you fly over cropland in the West on a clear summer day, you can see hundreds of green circles on the ground made by irrigation pivots. The abundant water really makes the corn grow.

Pivot

A crop sprayer has four tall wheels that help it roll through rows of plants growing up to six feet high. The computer in the sprayer cab controls the amount of spray applied to our crops. We scout the fields for pests and diseases before we spray. When we apply the proper type and quantity of chemicals, the plants are protected from insects and weeds.

Crop

Sprayer

Cutting hay is one of my favorite jobs on the farm. The alfalfa and clover blossoms smell heavenly. Haying used to be an all-summer job that included countless trips through the field to cut and process the hay. Now our mower-conditioner cuts, crushes, and piles the hay all in one pass.

Mower-

Conditioner

If the weather is sunny, we chop our hay the day after we cut it. The damp hay looks like grass clippings as it is blown into a wagon or truck. This "haylage" is dumped into a gigantic pile that grows like a green mountain out of nowhere. Then it is packed down and covered with white plastic to be saved for winter feeding.

Chopper

A combine looks like a small house moving across the land. This machine does several jobs at once. It cuts the corn, wheat, and oats. It beats the grain out of its husk. It blows the waste away and then transfers the grain to a grain box or hopper.

Combine

Where there are cows, pigs, or horses, there is manure. We spread all the manure from our cows onto the fields for fertilizer. Our spreader is pulled by a tractor. The spreader digs the manure right into the fields. The manure enriches the soil and helps our corn and hay to grow.

Manure

Spreader

Skid

Our skid steer is a miniloader that can turn on a dime and has bendable, jointed arms that attach to assorted buckets, forks, and scrapers. It hauls, cleans, and lifts. It spins, pushes, and pulls. We have two skid steers that are used all day, scooping feed and cleaning barns. They make our chores so much easier.

Steer

If Grandpa were here today, he'd be amazed at all the big machines we use to farm his land. I know he'd love to drive our skid steers, and he'd spend hours on our huge eight-wheeled tractor.

Today we grow over one thousand acres of crops, including corn, soybeans, and alfalfa. Whether we are plowing or planting, cutting or chopping, lifting or loading, there are machines for the job—machines Grandpa could never even have dreamed of.